ISBN: 978-1-7399188-3-5

Edited by E. Rachael Hardcastle
Formatted by E. Rachael Hardcastle
Written by Kate Ainsworth
Illustrated by Kate Ainsworth

Published by Curious Cat Books, United Kingdom
For further information contact www.curiouscatbooks.co.uk

First Edition

Poppy and Harvey
were out for the day,
off to the beach
for a swim and a play.

"You can't come with us Frank. I wish that you could.
Stay home, relax and remember to be good!"

With his family out, what could be the trouble,
at a playdate with Betsie to chase lots of bubbles?

He trotted to the garden and tapped on the fence.
"Come on now Betsie, don't keep me in suspense!"

A minute or two later, poking out from a hole.
Betsie the Bichon, tumbled out with a roll.

"Hello Mr Frank, would you look at the sun?
A beautiful day, perfect for some fun!"

"Yes," Frankie said,
"I have an idea,
the kids left their bubbles.
They're over here."

Bubble after bubble,
they blew and they popped.
It was so much fun,
they just couldn't stop!

Neither of them noticed,
the goblin in the tree,
giggling and grinning
with mischievous glee.

He tiptoed out,
when he knew they weren't looking,
and added a potion he'd been secretly cooking.

It was a magical potion
to make things grow.

He did it so quickly, they'd never know.

The next bubble they blew was two feet tall.
Betsie jumped forward and it swallowed her whole!

Up she was rising,
higher and higher.

"Eek!" shrieked Betsie
(she's not much of a flyer).

"Don't worry Betsie, we won't solve this alone."

Off Frankie scampered to fetch the 'Bone Phone'.

Who picked up first?
Why, Super Sausage Sid,
swiftly followed by the
Chihuahua called Kid.

"Disaster! We need you.
Betsie's in trouble!
She's trapped inside a
gigantic bubble!"

The whole crew assembled
in two minutes flat.

Frank had a plan.

"Well, thank
goodness for that!"

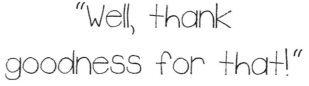

"We follow the bubble, wherever it goes,
and strap a long poker, to the end of Sid's nose".

"We'll give it a prick, as soon as we're near.
Then I will catch Betsie."

Sid gulped,
Oh dear!

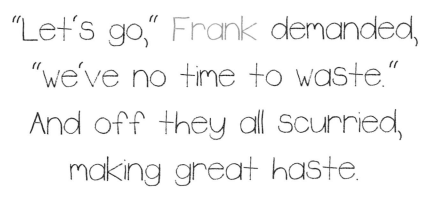

"Let's go," Frank demanded,
"we've no time to waste."
And off they all scurried,
making great haste.

The first thing they tried,
was a bunch of balloons.

But they sailed right past her...

...and crashed into the dunes.

The second attempt,
was almost successful.
But climbing a lighthouse
proved incredibly stressful!

"We've got one last shot to set Betsie free,
before that huge bubble
floats her straight out to sea."

"Let's head to the harbour, we need to be fast,
find the tallest ship and climb up the mast."

In no time at all
they'd scrambled aboard,
and pointed Sid's nose,
like the mightiest sword.

Along blustered Betsie, looking anxious and fraught.

She glanced down at Frankie, desperate to be caught.

All of them poised: "One, Two, Three!"

POP! went the bubble.

"Frankie, catch meeeeeeeeeeee!"

"Thank goodness, thank goodness.
It's over, hooray!
The Fabulous Mr Frank,
has saved the day!"

(Actually, we all know Sid
did most of the hard slog,
but Frank can sometimes
be such a diva dog.)

Back home, later on,
the kids rushed
through the door.

"Frankie, we missed you,
was your day a real bore?"

He responded with a snort,
a snuffle and a wiggle,
which we all know is 'dog'
for a jolly good giggle.

The many names of Mr Frank...

Author's Note

For my amazing Ma and Pa

Thank you for choosing my book.
I hope you've loved reading it.

This is book number 2 in the 'Fabulous Mr Frank' series.
For more information about my other books, please
visit: www.fabulousmrfrank.com.

God bless you all.

The original Mr Frank!

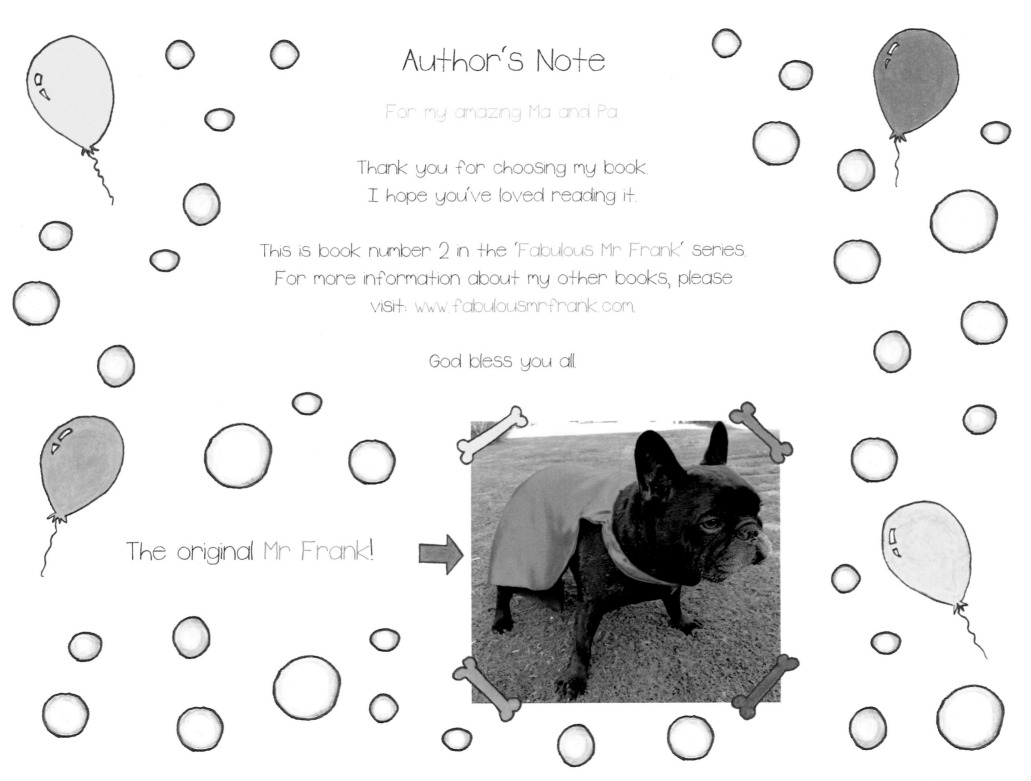

Lightning Source UK Ltd.
Milton Keynes UK
UKRC041234061222
413481UK00001B/1